Lyrics

Of My Heart

Jessica Spraggins

Copyright © 2017 Jessica Spraggins
All rights reserved.
Liberation's Publishing LLC ~ West Point, MS. 39773

ISBN13: 978-0-615-76642-3

Trust in the Lord with all thine heart; and lean not unto your own understanding. In all of your ways acknowledge him and he shall direct your paths.

Proverbs 3:5-6

Contents

- Our Father 3
- Daddy's little girl 4
- If These Walls Could Talk 5
- One Night Stand 7
- Unwise 9
- Just Friends 10
- Sweet Nothings 12
- If There Ever Were a Time 13
- Pure Intoxication 15
- Along Every Line of Love 16
- Somewhere, Somehow 18
- Woman Number Two 20
- Walk in Her Shoes 21
- Do My Heart A Little Justice 22
- My Heart vs My Mind 23
- Love Will Remain 25
- Fatal Love 26
- Love doesn't Happen That Way 28
- Paper and Pen 30
- What Happens? 32
- The Heart of a Woman 34
- Camouflaged 35

Poetry in Motion	38
You Light Up My Love	40
Midnight Love	41
Bedtime	42
How Could It Be	44
Don't Forget To Remember Me	46
My Favorite Hello	48
Cry My Love Away	49
Absence Makes the Heart Grow Fonder	52
Catchin' Feelins	54
Is Loving You Worth The Fight?	56
That's why I'm In Love with You	57
Love Has No Guarantees	58
Love Is a Battlefield	60
Grab My Notebook	61
Something is Missing	62
Sweetest Taboo	63
Same Thing That Makes You Laugh	64

Do not tell me what love is
Until you have truly lived it
"Love is not always patient and kind, love often comes with jealousy, anger, bitterness, and all manner of ugly things. That doesn't mean there is not beauty in it. Love is real. It is not a fairytale. It does not masquerade as utopia."

"Au contraire, the only thing I can tell you about love is that it is seldom perfect and the sooner you realize this, the sooner you'll find it"

-Samuel Decker Thompson
@aDudeWritingPoetry

Our Father

Our Father, which are in heaven
Hallowed be thy name
Trouble hearts and broken spirits
Got me realizing life ain't a game

She's strung out on cocaine
Because it helps ease the pain
Prostitution since adolescence
And even her soul feels no shame

His father has never been around
Has not one to hold him down
He turns to the streets for love
Now he's screaming, "Is there a heaven for a thug?"

Our father, which are in heaven
Hallowed by thy name
She cuts herself on the risk
Because she feels she's going insane

Raising her kids on her own
Because baby daddy decides to move on
Unprepared financially,
Hoping to be out of her misery
Is she really wrong?

Our Father….
Hallowed be thy name
Troubled hearts, broken spirits
Life surely aint a game

Daddy's little girl

She was only thirteen
She was daddy's little girl
She wished it was a dream
When daddy tore apart her world
Sneaking into her room
While her momma was asleep
Little girl, don't you moan
Little girl, don't you weep
She cried in hurt and disgust
As daddy told her to hush
She tried pretending its fine
While her heart piled with mistrust
Now it's night time again
And daddy comes in her room
She was daddy's little girl
From the day she came from the womb
Little girl, don't you moan
Little girl, don't you weep
Daddy said, "Don't say a word.
Just roll over and sleep

If These Walls Could Talk

If these walls could talk
Would they tell you all that they see
Would they silently stare
And become saddened like me

Would they speak on the girl
Using cocaine to stay sane
Neglecting the world around her
Just to ease up the pain

Would these walls cry out
At the dad abusing his girl
Got her growing up fast,
No ponytails just lush curls

Pimping her body for cash
Cause he's desperate and weak
His baby girl is just dying
Cause she sees him when she's sleep

Would these walls reach out
To the little boy on his grind
Thinking the street is his friend
Fast money corrupting his mind

Would the walls hold a blank stare
As the blood drips down her lips
She's his personal punching bag
And her body bag he will zip

Would they tell on the man
Who holds his wife tight at night
After sexcapades with young men
Lord knows that just aint' right

Her body flooded with HIV
Love has her living so blind
Wife of 23 years
Will the walls reveal his lie

Would they tell of affairs
And justified business flights
Six figure big business man
Whose wife cries to sleep every night

And what about her
And her nymphomaniac addictions
Lustful demons inside of her
Are her biggest convictions

Will the walls just cry out
They can't take all this rain
Will they take it all in
And collapse with the pain

One Night Stand

It all started from a simple kiss
Then on to a one night stand
Now I am in love with you
Wanting you to be my man

It was supposed to be nothing
We belonged to someone else
But what I felt when you kissed me
Was beyond anything I'd ever felt

Our kiss held so much chemistry
Our lovemaking combined our souls
And now your heart is my treasure
And this feeling is beyond my control

It started from a simple kiss
But grew into something strong
Letting you be my man
Will be so damn wrong

I can't stay away from you
Since that one night stand
I long for your touch and kisses
I wanna make you my man.

"When a man deceives me once
It is his fault
When twice; it is mines"

-George Horne

Unwise

I was considered unwise
Because I tried to revise
The character of his being
I didn't care to think with my head,
Just with my heart instead
Not realizing emotions are all so fleeing

I saw something quite different
In him he made me believe
That the love that I offered
He would greatly receive
But he scarred me,
Broke me badly...
I questioned God on my life
Pain tore me apart
The guy was not Mr. Right
I thought from heaven came
This man that I loved
In hindsight I see
We wasn't sent from above

I was considered unwise
Because I tried to revise
The character of his being
Not realizing emotions are all ever so fleeing

Just Friends

Maybe I'm a bit ahead of myself
To think this could be
To think that I could love you
And that you could love me

Both of us experiencing trust issues
Too afraid to give in
The universe demands, "Love each other!"
Our fears command "Just stay friends!"

I can't open myself to you
My heart has been failed before
I can't just walk away from you
You've become what my heart adores

Maybe I'm quite foolish
To think that this could be
Cause when I look in your eyes
They seem to truly love me

We both have issues with trust
We are both afraid to give in
The universe demands, "Love Each Other!"
Our fears command, "Just be friends

"Would you rather have love or trust"?

"Everyone wants someone that they can love and someone that will genuinely love them in return, but everyone needs someone that they can trust and someone that can trust them".

-Jessica Spraggins

Sweet Nothings

Come lay beside me
Let me whisper in your ear
You call it sweet nothings
I know it's what you want to hear

You smile as my words awaken your thoughts
Your mind becomes a rollercoaster
As I whisper sweet nothings to you
It obliges you to pull me closer

Embracing my every word
You are diggin' everything you heard
My poetic lines and captivating rhymes
Is everything that you preferred.

Now I've got you stirred
By whispering sweet nothings
It's not up for discussions
I see that you are blushing

Enhancing your mindset
To connect with mine
I'll capture your heart
Whispering sweet nothings, every, single, time.

If There Ever Were a Time

If there ever were a time I made you cry
And made you feel I did not care
If there ever were a time I told you lies
When I was supposed to be there

If there ever were a time
When my love proved untrue
If there ever were a time
I left you standing with no clue

If there ever were a time
I yelled and called you out your name
Made you feel so useless
It was impossible for you to remain

Maybe now my Karma is working on me
All the wrong I've done I'm starting to see

If there ever were a time I hurt you
But I didn't recognize
From the bottom of my heart I'm sorry.
I apologize.

"Words are Idle until someone gives them life."

-Jessica Spraggins

Pure Intoxication

You are like my favorite drug
I'm high, pure intoxication
Every little puff of you boy
Gives me a pure relaxation

Easin' my frustration
send me into another zone
Sippin' from your love
Has got me so gone

Am I wrong
For loving you like this
Something so bad feels so good
You gotta be high risk

But I insist
I can't even lie,
You got that fire
My strongest desire

Got my head in the clouds
Better than the finest wine
You're the strongest loud
Got me losing my mind

You are my favorite drug
I'm high pure intoxication
Sippin and puffin on you boy
Gives me liberation, pure relaxation

Along Every Line of Love

Promises that were not fulfilled
Truths that were never ever real
Hurts that bring about illness
And pains that even time would not heal

Cries that even the doves could not relate
Wounds that even gods could not take
Lying, infidelity, untruthfulness and cheating
Pressure that not ever peer pressure could make

Happiness that fades with the rays of sunshine
Sadness that stays until the end of time
Cloudiness that blinds what love should really be
Troubles that even a troubled man couldn't see

Along every line of love
Heartbreaks are in the process of taking place
Along every line of love
Sadness presides upon a happy face

It may feel like love is irreplaceable
Or that you are floating far above
But silence, heartbreak and isolation creeps in
Along every line of love

When love leaves, all is lost

-Jessica Spraggins

Somewhere, Somehow

Somewhere, Somehow
Things suddenly begin to change
Somewhere, somehow
My love became rearranged

Love doesn't abide like it used to
But it's only me not you
Somewhere, Somehow
My love became untrue.

Hold on to what's good for you
That's what momma would say
But the love I once felt in my heart
Has made me change my way

Up from the shadows of eternity
I promised you a lifetime
But our love somewhere, somehow
Has lost its lifeline

I have broken many promises
And made my love untrue
I know that it is not right
But sadly that is all I can give to you

Somewhere, somehow
My love began to change
Somewhere, somehow
My love has been rearranged.

"Women should come forward to protect other women, as only a woman can understand the problems of another one."

-Manju Warrier

Woman Number Two

I can't sit around and play your fool
I won't sit around and play role number two
What's the problem if you love me
What's holding you back if I love you

You claim you're in love with me
But you are there with her
Are you stringing me along
Is she what you prefer

Do I sit back and wait patiently
Till you decide where you wanna be
Or should I take the risk of someone
Else winning my heart
Because you are not embracing
What you say you feel for me

It seems as though it shouldn't be complicated
No areas of gray
But there's a three way love affair
And I ain't with the games you play

I love you so much
But I can't play your fool
I'm willing to bring you the stars and the moon
I just can't be woman number two

Walk in Her Shoes

The way you look at her
And tell her what you see
The way you talk to her
And tell her the things you once told me

The way you share your dreams with her
And whisper in her ear
The way you hold her in your arms
And shield her of her fears

The way you and her dance
To the invisible wind
I'll give everything and more
To walk in her shoes again

When you kiss her
It reminds me of how we used to be
When you hold her
I imagine how you once held me

I wish we could switch places
So I could feel your warmth again
When I see you with her
It reminds me of us-way back then
I know I hurt you
And without you my heart is blue
When I see you with her
I wish I could walk in her shoes

Do My Heart A Little Justice

Do my heart a little Justice
Serve and protect it just right
Make love to every fiber of my being
Romance me under the moonlight

Kiss me and hold me
Like it will be your last time
Love me like I'm all yours
And I'll love you like you're all mine

Do my heart a little justice
It's fragile, please do not break
Let's be fair in this crazy game
Crazy game of give and take

Embrace me like you'll love me forever
And show me I have nothing to fear
Promise me no matter what, you'll never leave
And that you'll always be near.

Do my heart a little justice
Serve it and protect it just right
Make love to every fiber of my being
And always kiss me goodnight

My Heart vs My Mind

There's this constant battle
Between my heart and my mind
Wanting to stay, knowing I should go
Trying to be patient, but instead wasting my time.

My heart and mind are at war
And my soul is not at peace
Why is this love shit so difficult
Do you even love me, at least

Trying to be understanding
To a situation that has no explanation
My energy loves you with everything it has
Yet and still you offer hesitation

I just need a little liberation
From this battle between my heart and mind
Wanting to stay, knowing I should go
Trying to be patient, but instead wasting time.

"Being deeply loved by someone gives you strength, while loving someone deeply gives you courage."

-Lao Tso

Love Will Remain

He loves me pass my hurt
And sees me for who I am pass my pain
He keeps his promises
Forever his love will remain

Is this all a dream
Often I have to pinch myself
Many times before love came
More times than many love has left

Caught up in a lover's bliss
I'm thanking God I finally found a love like this
Someone who adds spark to my soul
On the past, I refuse to reminisce
I don't have time to miss
What God has blessed me with

He loves me past my hurt
He sees me past my pain
Thank God, Love has conquered me
Thank God, this love will remain.

Fatal Love

The blood drips like streaming water
And her eyes are puffed up and red
The scratches outline the face of her
And the knots surround her head

The cries are distant sounds
That has the sound of the blues
But she's infatuated by love
And his false I love you's

Blood, sweat and tears
Isolated and alone
The feeling she thought was so right
Turned out to be so wrong

Destined to leave one day
If that day was not too late
The blood has destroyed her
And terminated her hopes and fate

She prayed for her soul mate
Someone special from above
But look at the blood and see the tears
This is only fatal love

Maybe I'm just a dreamer.
Momma said my head stayed up in the stars.
Maybe, just maybe, I am a fool
For wanting to love despite my scars.

-Jessica Spraggins

Love doesn't Happen That Way

I thought that because I wanted it so badly
That I would get an automatic love story
I thought I'll get someone to send me just because flowers
And kiss my forehead every morning
And tell me not to worry

I thought that I'll meet my prince charming
And happily ever after we would be
And no matter how many women came across his vision
I'll be the only woman he could ever see
But sadly, love doesn't happen that way
Maybe I wanted the love I saw on T.V

The kind that makes butterflies dance in your tummy
But love doesn't work that way, it's quite funny

Instead of sharing our dreams and passions
We fought and drove each other insane
We cried, there was blood sweat and tears
We yelled and called each other names

We played the game of "tick for tack"
Instead of being forgiving, turning the other cheek
Instead of playing for keeps
We made each other weak

**Throughout this journey
I've learned one thing on this day
Hopes of the moonlit and romantic walks
Love just doesn't happen that way…**

Paper and Pen

Maybe this is a bit old fashioned
As my thoughts lead me to paper and Pen
But my heart has been having conversations
With my mind
By you being the topic, I want to let you in.

Now I could let my love remain a mystery
And not let you know exactly what I feel
I ain't interested in wasting your time
Nor playing with your mind
Because my love could come off to be surreal

But somewhere down the line
You enticed my mind
You opened my heart
And tore down walls over time

Parts of my love for you
I want to hold in captivity
But because you spark my curiosity
I want to give you every inch of me

But eventually, I feel that
These feelings too will fade
If we ain't on the same page
It'll just be a game of charades.

So should I let you invade my thoughts?
Should I open my mind to let you in?
I think I'll stick to being old fashioned

And leave my thoughts with the paper and pen

What Happens?

What happens when we both get tired of trying
When I no longer make you happy and I'm
constantly seeing you crying

What happens when our love turns into hate and
whether we want to be together becomes a debate
Because right now our love is in a dead state
Loving you feel so wrong
our hearts no longer relate

The divine love we once shared has become of
destroyed fate

So what happens when our love fails,
when what we have fought so hard to build together
no longer prevails

What happens in that moment
Do we just decided to let go
Do we throw everything away
When our love decides to outgrow

Just to know…
That there's a possibility of someone holding you
Makes me wonder
If our love was ever true

So what happens when we decide to stop trying and
call everything to quits
If I continue to love you

I feel it will be too big of a risk

So I'll just walk away now
Since we are no longer trying
I'll just walk away now
To prevent you from crying

The Heart of a Woman

She never stopped loving
Although her heart has been damaged over the years
She always felt the need to protect those she love
Although she carried her own personal fears

She has cried tears that only God could wipe away
Yet she fills laughter throughout the universe
And although her heart was there to nurture and love
It sometimes seemed her blessing was her curse

She bears children, take care of homes
Sometimes raised children all alone
Her clothing was dipped in confidence and strength
Even when her heart sung sad songs

Her heart has been bruised
From the ways of a wicked world
But the Heart of a Woman
Always carries the spirit of a little girl

When God created her heart
It was designed with courage and grace
It was His summon
That she be beautifully designed...
The Heart of a Woman

Camouflaged

You asked me what I expected
And I told you what to expect
You played your cards right
You expected to get me naked

Using your charm and your wit
To play the game of manipulation
Just so you can lay with me
And indulge in sexual relations

You camouflaged yourself
As a source of stability and protection
Just so you could fill me up with sweet lies
And a hard erection

Instead of telling me what you truly came for
You became what I wanted you to be
Just so you can feel like a man
And say that you lay with me

But you played with me
Enticed my mind for your own
Sexual fantasies

Surely I was a ton of naïve
To believe or fall for the lies
But the master of manipulation
Always has the best disguise

So in my eyes

You were one of the best that came along
You blamed me for falling for the game
You feel you did no wrong

But to you it was only a game
A game of camouflage
But once again I have to deal with another betrayal;
Sabotaged

The world has the power to break or make you
To make you bitter or beautiful
Will you remain a caterpillar
Or develop into a butterfly."

-Jessica Spraggins

Poetry in Motion

Often I behave in a free or uninhibited way
Cause' baby I ain't afraid to let my hair down
There's some diamonds meeting at my thighs, starlight in my eyes
I'm full of confidence so sashaying is just the way I walk round.

I hold my head up like I'm having conversations with the cloud
But blame my momma for that
Because she raised me to be proud.

I say what I mean and I mean what I say
And no I won't apologize if I offend you in any way
Just charge it to my head and not my heart
I've been judged, lied on, talked about and betrayed
But strong women don't fall apart.

So I'll continue to strut around
Like I'm the only girl round town
I'm not cocky, overly confident
There's just a spirit in me that can't be broken, only bent.
So to no extent
Will I play by your rules
I am a woman of poetry
My heart sings no blues

So when you look at me
There is no need to be confused

I am all woman, the perfect potion
Hips twisting like a drop of hip hop
I am Poetry in Motion.

You Light Up My Love

You light up my love
Every time you come around
The physical Chemistry is in full effect
So we both know what's going down

You looking at me
And I'm staring at you
We both can read each other's thoughts
So we don't have to give no clue

My heart no longer sings the blues
Instead boy it dances to your beat
You light my soul on fire
And you make my legs weak

In between the sheets
Our moans are in tune
Our bodies harmonize in the sweetest way
It's like music that fills the room

Every time we are away
It's you I anticipate
My body speaks your love language
It's only you I can relate

Is this some type of Karmic Energy
Or is it just a strange chemistry
Maybe its heaven sent from above
Because boy you light up my love.

Midnight Love

It's a little pass midnight
The stars and moon are having conversations
The clock screams out "tick tock"
And my body yearns for sexual relations

As I lay there-I patiently wait for you
I can feel my temperature rise
I want us to savor each other's love
As I wrap you in my legs in between my thighs
Pushing you deeper into my love
You stare passionately into my eyes
Our bodies are n perfect harmony
No secret, no games, no lies

Our bodies are intertwined
The connection is so divine
I moan in sweet ecstasy
As you enter me from behind-
But I don't mind
Because your love strokes are love filled
You are giving my body the chills
Taking me higher with sexual thrills.

As the clock screams "tick tock"
My climax sends me far above
My body is in a total bliss
Because of this midnight love

Bedtime

When the world is quiet
And alone does the world seem
I lay peacefully at bedtime
Where you are a part of my dream

When the entire world is sleeping
I imagine us being together
At night, at bedtime
I pray for us to be forever

I imagine us dancing under the stars
And making love under the moon
At bedtime, my imagination consist of
Us being together soon

I hear your whispers
They feel like a night summers breeze
I can feel you touching me
Which brings about much ease

No matter what
You constantly stay on my mind
You lying next to me
While I lay peacefully at bedtime

"We are all on a journey to find something. Quite often while we search for that something that we are missing, we lose ourselves….and before we know it…we are in too deep"

-Jessica Spraggins

How Could It Be

How could it be so easy to walk away
When my love commands you to stay
How could you allow someone to take my place
How could I be so easy to erase

I gave you every part of me
Down to the very core
And you turned and betrayed my love
And pushed it right out the door

How could you risk losing me
When I gave you everything
Was everything we shared a lie
Because that's how things seem

Or is this a bad dream
Somebody please awaken me
Questioning myself what I did wrong
To make you wanna move on

Was it really that easy to walk away
My love commanded you to stay
How could I be so easy to erase
How could you let someone take my place

Although it has been hurt, bruised, and damn near broke there is strength in me that refuses to give up and a courage that denies the right to give in. There is a power so passionate and fierce that lives deep with me that no matter what may come as a challenge or a defeat I will fight. I will win. I will conquer. Call it whatever you please but I call it. The Heart of a Woman...

-Jessica Spraggins

Don't Forget To Remember Me

When she doesn't cater to your every need
And make love to you selflessly
Do me one little favor boy
Don't you forget to remember me

When she doesn't hold you down like a King
And stick by your side like a queen
Don't you dare fail to realize
That at one time, we were a good team

But you began to sell me dreams
And all of your lies I refused to buy
So we parted ways, hours turned to days
And our hearts no longer wanted to try

For months you had my mind in a whirlwind
Over the heartbreak and deceit
But you will never find another lover
No other woman could compete

Bridges were burned, tables were turned
Maybe Karma will have you to see
That my love is one in a million
So don't you forget to remember me.

Emphasize

I can't emphasize nor describe
The way you make me feel
Neither can I explain the way
Your lovemaking gives me the chills
Should I remind you of how your love brings me thrills
I know what I feel for you is way pass real.

You have got my head in the stars
Just because of the person you are
You have got me infatuated with you boy
And I'm delighted thus far
I can't begin to explain
How excited I get just at the mention of your name
And boy you stay on the brain
And it's such a shame
How you stay on my mind
I can't emphasize or describe
The way you make feel
But maybe in due time
You'll know my love is real

This jones in my bones
I so desperately wish you could feel
From the top of my head to the bottom of my heel.
I can't begin to describe or put into words to emphasize
The way your love has got me gone
Boy, I'm so mesmerized

My Favorite Hello

"Hello, how are you?"
I smile when you walk my way
You are my favorite Hello
And you brighten up my day

Even if I were Ray Charles
I would still be able to see
The way you light up my world
The way you compliment me

But there's this disconnect that I feel
Every time you are not near
It's like my heart has an absence of its left ventricle
Every time you are not here

Being apart from you too long
Makes my blissful soul cry
You are my favorite hello
Yet, my hardest goodbye

Cry My Love Away

I've tried to talk to you
So that we can both have an understanding
I've planted kisses on your forehead
So that my love wouldn't come off to be so demanding

I've raised my tone, even though it was wrong
Trying to get through to you
That my love is for real, is true

I've lain in bed plenty of nights
Heartbroken and alone
While you were out on the streets
On the streets, on the roam
Trying to let you be a man
And find your own way
But what do I do when my love has no more fight?
And my words have nothing more to say?

I've shown you I'll be there no matter what
I got your back no if's and's or but's
You constantly hurt me, take my love lightly

Is my love not enough for you
Why isn't it me that you choose
Why after I have loved you so strong
You go and give my heart the blues
Got me feeling misused and abused
Lonely and confused
I've fussed and I've fought

Now there's nothing else to say
Now my tears take the place of my words
I'll just cry my love away

"To want to share someone's happiness
That's admiration
To want to share someone's pain and sorrow
Now, that's love.

-Jessica Spraggins

Absence Makes the Heart Grow Fonder

They say it's absence that makes
The heart grow fonder
But it's your captivating presences
That makes my heart wonder
I can't help but look into your eyes and ponder
Because baby boy you are all I see
And I know your love is written all over me.

I miss you when you are away
And I wish that you could stay
But oh the way you make me feel when you're near
You light up my day
In a major way.

I can't really go on to explain
The passion that I have for you
When you call my name
Baby boy you drive me crazy
Although I like to think I'm sane

I don't mean to sound vain
When it comes to your love
I ain't trying to butter you with flattery
But you gotta be sent from above
Cause' your love is like a glove
Because it fits me to the T
It's more than chemistry
It's something deeper I see

The way you fill me up
You never let me down
They say it's absence that makes the heart grow fonder
But baby boy my love is intrigued when you are around

Catchin' Feelins

Unconditional love has been demolished
Because we live in a "love em leave em" society
Trust and love are only words of emotions
Which forces me to keep my sobriety
I can't hold him down as a man
And he can't lift me up as a woman
Because we confuse date night with chillin'
So we are left with torn emotions and mixed feelins'

Relationships are turned into situationships
Communication and conversations don't exist
Something as beautiful and pure as true love
Has been categorized as being high risk
But I do not fail to admit
That love can be quite risky
But what if it works out for the better
You gotta look at the possibility of infinity

Not really knowing where we stand with each other
Our relationships ain't solid built
On what's real with one another
So instead of getting to know and trying to grow
We just kick it and chill and chump the deuces up
When emotions come in to play
And we start to "feel"
Maybe this generation is exempt from the present of
life and love
Because instead of dating
And building something real
We find it easier to be "just chillin"

And then we are left vulnerable "just catchin feelins"

Is Loving You Worth The Fight?

Sometimes I sit and question
If loving you is worth the fight
If I never give up on us
Would my love make things right
I fall down on my knees with a broken heart
And ask God for some insight
No matter how many times you wronged me
Am I a fool to wanna love you in spite
Maybe I'm a bit naïve
Because my heart wants to believe
That if I never take my love away
Your love I can achieve
But is loving you worth the fight
When my very soul starts to grieve
One part of me wants to stay
And part of me wants to leave
Sometimes I sit and question
How long will I have to fight
Would this beautiful struggle last a lifetime
How long will it take to make it right

That's why I'm In Love with You

It's challenging-
Sometimes I even wanna call it quits
But I must admit
That I'm profound of a love like this
They say that opposites attract
And that has got to be true
You dot my I's and cross my T's
Maybe that's why I'm in love with you
You are nothing like what I'm use too
No foot massages after a long day of work
Instead, when I want to be held and caressed
You go on and act like a jerk
When I need someone to share that they care
You are hard as a rock; no empathy
In times of misfortune, pitfalls and all
You are not my source of sympathy
But for all of the handful of times
You hold me in your arms
I'm reminded of how much you love me
And how you will protect my heart from all harms
But our love is quite demanding
Dotting my I's and crossing my t's are the thing that you do
I guess that's why no matter how hard it gets
I'm still in love with you.

Love Has No Guarantees

I know that love has no guarantees
But my heart longs for you to stay
I need your long lasting promises
That our love will never fade away
And if there is ever a day
That I make you feel as though you can't stay
Promise that we can sit down and work it out
Until we find a better way
I know love has no guarantees
But let's agree to disagree
That no matter how hard it gets
That we will never set each other free
Instead I just need you to love me
And you willingly let me do the same
I know that this love thang
Can be hard to tame
Forever and always, until the end of time
Let's explore the possibility
Let's kiss on you loving me
Although I know love has no guarantees.

"Love is a Battlefield"

-Jessica Spraggins

Love Is a Battlefield

It started out as arguments
Disagreeing with each other's point of views
The physical expression of love we made last night
Turned into verbal "I hate you's"

Now we are prepared for war
Blood, sweat, and tears
Momma told me love is a battlefield
So put aside all of your fears
Instead put on your shields
In love and war prepare to guard your heart
Because on these battlegrounds
You can easily be torn apart.

Instead of sitting down like adults
We imprisoned each other, no liberation
Instead of talking things through
Social media got more attention than the situation
There was nothing but hesitation and frustration
When it came to working things out
We yelled and we shouted
When there was nothing to yell and shout about

As we both prepared for war
I knew this love would go downhill
It's war time, blood shed, broken hearts
Love is surely a battlefield

Grab My Notebook

(Inspired by Paper and Pen)

What am I to do
When my heart begins to fall for you
Do I tell you how I feel
And risk being rejected
Do I let go and open up
And risk being neglected
See I've tried this love thing before
It left me feeling a bit confused
So am I wrong for not letting go
Simply because I don't wanna get used
See, I really don't wanna lose
With this thing we call love
But boy you got me addicted to you
As if you're my favorite kind of drug
I want to express to you how I feel
And let you know what's real
But even when my heart wants to speak
My words just keep still
So damn, I guess I'll just keep quiet
Maybe I shouldn't hold it in
What's a girl to do besides write about it
I'll grab my notebook and my pen

Something is Missing

There is this strange void that we possess
Something in our love is missing
Maybe we spend too much time fighting
And not enough time kissing

Now you have got me reminiscing
On the good times that we share
When the laughter outweighed the tears
When I knew you really cared

But now things are bittersweet
Got me thinking can things continue to be
Although you tell me the love is genuine
There's something different I see

There's a strange void between us
And surely something is missing
We spending too much time fighting
And not enough time kissing

Sweetest Taboo

It's not Molly or Ecstasy
Neither is it cocaine
It's not Paul Masson nor Patron
That makes it hard for me to maintain

You should be prohibited
Better yet boy, maybe even restricted
Because you have got to be some sort of taboo
The way you got me addicted

I'm conflicted, because I'm trying to resist it
But I can't quite let go
The harder I try to walk away
I feen for you even mo'

Although I am a woman of control
I think I'm losing myself
When I think of your smile I wanna stay for a while
I wanna give you all of me until there's no more left

It may seem like a bad thing
The way you got my head gone
But the love that you give
Makes my life worth the live
And you're so good it can't be wrong

This taboo is so damn strong
I don't wanna let go, I gotta hold on
Because baby boy, there is no question that it is you
Who has become my sweetest taboo

Same Thing That Makes You Laugh

It started off
All fun and games
The trips and passionate lovemaking
And the cute puppy names
We would sit and talk about everything
Our love was brand new
Obviously, you were all into me
And I was all into you.

We dated and we cuddled
I often fell asleep in your arms
You were my liability and my security
You kept me safe from all harms
But in the blink of an eye
I'm sitting here trying not to cry
My mind is going in all directions
As I sit and question myself why

Sitting here listening to love songs
Intellectually trying to piece shit together
How together forever
Drastically turned into never
Where did the lying come into place
Where did the games come from
How did I go from wholeheartedly loving you
To feeling broken and numb

What does she have, that I didn't

Why did I play the game of revenge
It seems just yesterday we were in love
But now we're not even friends
Momma warned me about this
And surely it was no lie
That the same thing that makes you laugh
Will be the same thing that makes you cry

www.ingramcontent.com/pod-product-compliance
Lightning Source LLC
Chambersburg PA
CBHW062028290426
44108CB00025B/2826